D1522830

If you meet Harrison's Basho on the road, kill him. Then steal his poems.

— *Bob Tisdale*

Outrageously amusing. Basho should be on every poetry lover's late-night show.

—*Jane Spiro*

Basho bursts the Zen balloon — or at least the pretentiousness of it Western incarnations — with pin-pricking wit.

— *John Daniel*

Say goodbye to the pharmaceuticals. These poems are the best anti-depressant in the store. And the new pieces continue the magic of the original.

—*Alan Spurgeon*

He trips you by the heels on every page. An amazing book. And very funny.

— *Elise Hardin*

Eliot, Berryman, Olson, Bly, Ginsberg — and much else — are targets in this hilarious, good-humored spoof. I've rarely read anything so enjoyable.

— *Elizabeth Moreley*

Harrison's Basho is the modernist trickster. Just when you think he's serious he turns 180, and is full of drollery. And then, the opposite. There's nobody quite like him. When I first heard him on the radio he had me laughing all around the house.

— *Colby Borkman*

If we were to believe the *The Basho Poems* are nonsensical we might end up red-faced. Underneath some of the most beguiling and charming poetry you can find a highly perceptive and innovative intelligence is waiting to be read and enjoyed. Because Harrison understands the literary canon, and because we know that he understands, these poems alert the reader to many playful possibilities. They shine with superb craftsmanship, and sing with rebellion and beauty. Harrison doesn't just describe, he makes you see, and at times he is mind-bendingly funny. Surreal as Magritte, the words work upon the sensibility as a watermelon on a hot day works upon the tongue. Just when you think poetry has exhausted its surprises, along comes an original book like *The Basho Poems*, a book you'll want to read aloud, and to share with friends.

— *Robert Drummond*

William Blake: "If the fool would persist in his folly he would become wise." Wise guy Keith 'Basho' Harrison: "Been there. Done that."

— *Eric Nelson*

Also by Keith Harrison

POETRY
Points in a Journey
Songs from the Drifting House
The Basho Poems
A Burning of Applewood
Words Against War

LIMITED EDITIONS
Two Views from a Window
A Town and Country Suite
The Sense of Falling

TRANSLATIONS
At the Wedding of Peleus and Thetis:
Catullus #64 (with Linda Clader
Sir Gawain and the Green Knight
(The Folio Society & Oxford World's Classics)

PLAYS
The Water Man
The Papers of Lady Ann Vaughn
Richard and Fredrika

TEXT
How to Stop Your Papers from Killing You
(and Me)

FORTHCOMING
CHANGES: New & Collected Poems, 1962-2002
Not Quite Ithaka: Encounters on the Way

The Complete Basho Poems

Keith Harrison

BLACK
WILLOW
PRESS

Northfield

ISBN No. 0-939394-09-X

The Complete Basho Poems

Keith Harrison

ACKNOWLEDGMENTS

Some of these poems have appeared in the *Carleton Miscellany* and *25 Minnesota Poets* (Minneapolis, The Nodin Press)

Some were broadcast on several programs of the A.B.C. (Sydney and Melbourne) in 1975 and 1976.

My warm thanks, once again, to Elizabeth Edwards for the title design of the Nodin Press edition of *The Basho Poems*, which we have modified slightly for the cover of this book, and to Mark Heiman for his skill, good humor and industry in re-setting the whole text of the poems for this new edition.

AUTHOR'S NOTE

The first edition of the Basho poems was printed in a
limited edition of 200 copies, hand-set by Lissa Lunning
at the Cyathus Press, Iowa City (1975). That edition is
now out of print. A trade edition, published by the Nodin
Press, Minneapolis (1981) is also out of print.

This new gathering includes two longer pieces written
subsequent to the appearance of those earlier editions so
that, with this publication, all the Basho poems are now
between two covers.

CONTENTS

THE BASHO POEMS

(1972 & 1981)

for Arthur Gropen,
and for the taxi-driver in Washington, D.C.
who set me laughing

BASHO BESIDE THE MOUNTAIN

There was this message
From K'en Lee's nephew to his father's brother—
Or was it to his father's brother's wife?
Walking beside the mountain,
It occurred to him that he was very small
And somewhat stupid.

★

The mountain watched him as he moved:
Slow dot around the giant base.

★

A cormorant pierced the smooth
Silk-sheen of water under the mountain.
Basho held his breath, went down with him
Down and down, hunting.
His head began to pound. Red-faced
He suddenly blew it all out.

It's clear I could never be a cormorant, he said.

★

Basho flopped down
On a rustic bridge. There were a few
Fat carp dodging among the weeds.
K'en Lee's nephew came by.

Why are you looking down with such intensity—
Do you seek Enlightenment in water?

Neck's tired, Basho said—
Been looking too long
At that bloody mountain.

*

When the harlot confronted Basho
Her jasmine smell almost undid him.
As they undressed he was amazed
At the loveliness of her flanks, the way
Her small breasts bobbled when she laughed.
There are two kinds of harlot, Basho said.
For the first I have the images of
Spring water pelting over rocks,
A gazelle, a pitcher brimming with honey.
And for the second?

I find it difficult to think about such people, Basho said.

Then he pinned her to the mountain.
All afternoon.

Afterward it was very simple.

There was the mountain over them, and under them.
There was the bellsound winding over the lake.
And there was jasmine.

*

At about the fortieth twist
In the mountain road
A drunken bandit came at him.
Empty your pockets, he said.

I'm a poet, Basho said.
I live off other people's money.

The bandit lunged at him.

 Basho kicked him in the cods. Stalked on.

★

Very well, I'll tell you the Thousand Things, said Basho.

There's bird's wing, the smell of it,
There's the grain of rice that eats you,
Jasmine petals on the executioner's sleeve.
There's knock of water against the keel, the drum at
the center

Certain wines whose bouquets drift into eternity.

There's also rock which is what it is,
The uncommitted bandit who is what he is not
There are dragons that seem mountains
And mountains that seem dragons

And finally, there's the mountain.

That's not a thousand!

Damn right it is, said Basho. Count them again.

★

Basho's wife said:
Where have you been all day?

Pinning a harlot to the mountain.

You, bag of bones? Your head's so full of dreams
You couldn't tell a woman from a turkey.

Perhaps it was the jasmine, Basho said.

But his wife, stirring a pot, didn't hear him.

★

After his descent from the mountain
Basho wrote three poems.
The poems were:

(1)   A wind-blasted gull
   Grips the
   Crow's nest:
   The pine bends as the earth
   Hog-rolls.

(2)   Moonlight
   Floods my window:
   If a friend looks in tonight
   He'll darken me.

(3)   Unbroken light on the lake.
   The cormorant's hunting.
   Heavens, four hours!

Basho read these poems to his wife.

   Nothing important
   Can be done
   In seventeen

   Syllables, she said.

THE THING DIRECT

REPLY TO THE GRAMMARIANS

I am a knockabout man of little learning
And almost nothing that will pass for tact.
I like the thing direct: the wolf's wet fang,
Howl of a new-born pig. Appetite. Fact.
The soft *plop* of plum-falls in October
's my kind of music either drunk or sober.
Against the tune that your grammarians sing
I set the landscape of the pigeon's wing.
You who stand back and crookedly explain
Can never quell this hunger in my brain.

HANGOVER POEM

Must've been the sakë
Immature and sour, that
We drank together:
The mind beneath my hat
Flicks about like a feather,
But cannot find its bird.

QUICK SHADOW

Strolling in the garden
Comes to spires of lettuce, tall as himself.
A pear-tree snapped by the wind
Sags over the ruined cabbages.
He looks up.
A shadow moves across the mountain
Very quickly.

He shivers,
Trundles his clanking bones indoors.

SKETCH FOR AN AESTHETIC

If a man is intent on writing,
Basho remarked to a stupid cousin,
He has to study details:
Color of a tiger's belch, the way
Wind wobbles
Before it polishes the pomegranates,
The shape of adverbs in sultry weather;
You also have to understand
The irrationality of water;
How it behaves when you kick it.

When you come to the end of all that
You have to study Man,
The creature whose defining virtue's
To bite the same behind that he tries to sit on.

HE RECAPITULATES/FORECASTS
THE STAGES OF HIS LIFE

Three Minutes Before Birth

Someone poured cold water on my toe.
Insulted, I drew it back, decided
To stay inside.

At Three

A fat fish stood up
Suddenly out of the pool
And flapped himself
Into the sun.

At Fourteen

I begin to understand calligraphy.
From this moment I will be lost.

At Twenty

Blasted with love's excess
I plunge down the mountain
And break my ankle in a ditch.

At Thirty

Whatever engine is running me, it
Missed a stroke. There, on the
Wet roadway, as I looked at the clouds bunched up,
The blank water.

At Forty

If the evil persists at this time
Good may never be at hand.

At Fifty

'Lotus blossoms on smooth water . . .'

At Sixty

'Smooth water . . .'

At Seventy

Lubricious fantasies. The last
Twitch, the first
Twitch.

HIS TRANSMIGRATIONS

TRAVELING TOWARD
THE VACHE QUI PUE RIVER
or
Basho Attempts to Translate Robert Bly

I am walking very slowly across Minnesota
Inside a car with no engine and no seats.
I have left the seats in a hundred country towns
And the old squat around on them and dream
Of onions. In country towns
Sitting down is never the same as standing.
It is dusk but I have forgotten why.
It is also Minnesota, whatever that means.

The moon floats out of the turkey sheds
Dragging the turkeys and their smells with it.
The soybeans are myopic, you can hear them
Sulking and kicking each others' shins.
The lamplight collapses on the grass
Like a spavined frog.

Suddenly the moon flaps past
And smashes itself against the box-elder.
Wearing my bottomless car I slouch over a bridge
And listen with unspeakable sympathy
While two Aquarians try to screw their boat to the river.
I teach them a chorus of the *Vache Qui Pue,* and they
Unscrew the boat. They have never heard
Of Missoula, Montana, where I was happy.

BASHO REJECTS HINDUISM
or
Marshall McLuhan in India

tat tvam asi

tas tati mav

masa tat vit

ma's a tit vat

's i'm a tat vat

(a titva tat, 'm?)

vatsit mata

ta ma, vat's it!

'tat tvam asi' = TAT AM I.

VAST

AS T.V.

BASHO'S MARGINAL SONGS

Happy Day Among the Elephant People
Father, blubber, grease body
Tumbling through the sky.

'The earth is very peculiar.'

The Sage Who Came by While Basho
Was Trying to Restore His Rotten Pear-Tree
I met a man who lived too long;
This was the burden of his song,
Frog's breath, bird-lime, blow on your twisted nail.

I met a man who lived too slow
Seventy years as these things go
His eye turned in and his tooth yellow.

Both long and slow died in a fog
(Two withered tails who'd lost their dog)
One frozen hard beside a log—
One falling far, very rapidly.

He Rebukes His Underwear
Fortnightly.
Fought nightly.

Late Breakfast
Bean curd
Bean herd
Been heard
Been turd
Been had
Absurd
Merd

The Crocodiles Who Stayed Too Long

Whatever the fig meant
Was no figment

Whatever the pig lent
Was no pigment payment

Whatever the horses say
There was no horseplay

There were only the spaces, where they'd
                                    thrashed about.
The ashes, the bleeding petals, the debris.

Railroad Tanka

I walk the gleaming rails
Ahead of me
Two feet
Above the black horizon
The full moon thunders toward me.

Minnesota Winterdrive

I said to them that this was all the time hardly even moving
you have this huge back of the beast I said a million miles
in any direction are all the same with the road winding
through our eyes and out the back of our heads always
I said this is always and no way out of it road road road
and any direction of snow snow west and snow snow east
where if any god has a hot body he doesn't put his bum
down here I said the sun goes five months inside and it
stays inside like a cinnamon bear in a hole I said they said
why don't you give over you go on too much I said this is
a road road oh yes this is a road and what you think you
can do about it with all the driving it all just stays the same
big fat blackwhite beast like the backside of Betelgeuse all
ahead of us and all around and the cold sun crouching in
his hole I said they said Jesus belt up get him out of here I
said laughing like hell I said you can't even stop this is the
road road this is the road.

Basho in Melbourne

I walk through the long suburbs questioning.

No one replies.

SEVEN DREAM POEMS

1

I am in bed with a harlot. We are both covered in sprays
of jasmine. There are so many flowers that I cannot find
the harlot. An eagle, balanced on the bed-stead points a
red beak down at us. I leap up and strangle it and hurl
its hot body down into the market place. When I turn
round the harlot has gone, though on the heaped flowers
she has left a discreet white card. I turn the card over.
It is blank on both sides. I stand there shivering, covered
with eagle feathers.

2

This time I am inside a jasmine flower. A procession of dead people go by, carrying bootlaces in their right hand. In the other hand they hold flags inscribed with an indecipherable message. They begin to whirl the bootlaces rapidly. They make a noise like a thousand bull-roarers. A dead arm cracks off like a limb from a plaster doll and crashes into the foliage beneath my hideout. I crawl deeper into the flower.

3

The bowl of a brilliantly lacquered lute presses into my belly and begins humming as the wind drives through it. I tune it with my toes. Aha, it sings like a turtle! I rub a leg experimentally across the strings. At first nothing happens, then the hairs get caught and it hurts like hell. I wake my wife up with the shouting.

4

I am rowing a huge black bull across the lake. The bull snuffs the air and wheels forward like a dolphin. I throw back my head, warrior-style and shout *Grah, Grah* into the waves. A storm beats up and we barrel through the black waves singing together. Suddenly there is a haven of sunlight and calm water. My wife has laid out the breakfast in a little bay. There are plates of wild honey and sherbet and a tiny salad of frogs' legs doused in wine. All the plates are floating on lotus leaves. The bull noses among them delicately. Kingfishers flash emerald and scarlet, then dissolve in air. Astride the bull I eat with aristocratic nonchalance. My wife prepares more dishes on the shore.

5

A line of soldiers plunges down the mountain, beating
drums, dislodging stones. They break down my door and
ram me against the wall.

— Where are all your filthy poems? the leader asks.
— Over there, in that bowl of moonlight.

They smash the bowl and hand the poems round. The
soldiers eat them. When they've finished the leader leaps
at me and yells into my face WE WANT MORE.

—There aren't any more, you evil-smelling bastard.

I try to kick him but my boot turns into a swan.

6

I write a perfect poem which gathers itself together and walks off the page with a light sneeze. It goes outdoors and squats under the pear-tree. I can hear it talking to the lettuce.

7

A chess-board. Myself against my brother. The kings are
taken and only two pieces are left on the board — both
white, both pawns. They are on the same file, with one
square between them. We shout obscenities about who
should move. My wife rushes in and angrily sets the
pieces alongside each other. We take each other *en passant*.
Then we re-arrange the board. Each player now has
half the black and half the white pieces. What delicious
complications! We play on serenely.

BASHO DEVISES HIS OBITUARIES

1

The poet Basho is dead. A light has gone out, a gloom has settled on the land. From hundreds of miles the mourners troop toward his tomb, his verses resounding in their hearts. One man, crazed with sorrow, walked off the road and, losing his way in a marsh, drowned himself. There is no end to the sorrow. The governor has sent out functionaries to keep the farmers at their work. But still they leave the fields.

The career and person of Basho are swaddled in enigma. Even those who thought they knew him well find him elusive. On the face of it his life was exemplary. He kept a garden. By habit he rose early, sharpened his pencils and wrote till noon. In the afternoon, fatigued by the labor of composition, he slept. His life was of a simplicity that flowed in everything he touched. Apart from a single indiscretion on the mountain he was faithful, diligent, clear-headed, robust, manly, majestic in purpose, forbidding in repose—and without question he was the best poet in the largest village of the region.

Basho was the ghost in all of you. In a world of complex sewers he asserted the radical normality of trees and pigeons. He understood the quality of metals and the delicate grain of amethyst and agate. The unctuous plumage of the crow, the taste of wild berries, the flesh of women were a language to him. He spent his life trying to translate that language and, once or twice, succeeded. Misunderstood in his life, he now begins his long dialogue with creatures underground. If he can persuade them, maybe they will lift him out so that, once again, he can plunge his head into a spray of blossoms and run his words like fingers through the warm fur of the world.

2

When Basho awoke in his bed
And found he was bloody near dead
He cried out in wonder
'I've made a huge blunder—
I had such a good line in my head.'

He took up his pen in a flash
And slumped at his desk with a crash
When a harlot appeared
And seductively leered.
Her visit quite settled his hash.

3

I knew him quite well in his younger days. Frankly, I
thought he was a mean little sod. Stuck-up. Enormous
opinion of himself. He hated what our group was doing
because most of us were writing better than he was. I
liked some of the early things, but after forty he started to
write reams of inane pap and all that stuff about pigeons
and jasmine. God, who needs it? My own theory is that
he was an old lecher posing as a poet — you know,
the grave look toward the distant mountains, the sigh of
impatience at a question which he thought beneath him.
Most of the time he was just too dense to understand.

Most of all he was cruel and ruthless. Do you know that
one time up on the mountain he just lashed out and
kicked an old farmer in the groin? And then he went
around spreading this story about how he was attacked
by a bandit. My God, no self-respecting bandit would
go near Basho. You could see straightaway that he was
penniless. And he'd been wearing the same robe for
about forty years, and it stank.

4

All my life I have been afraid of death. I persuaded
myself that the thought of death was boring—the hand
hesitating over the page, a vision of rats and skulls. Such
things keep a man from his business, I thought. To make
a small thing well a man needs joy. And who can be
joyful when his head is full of death?

And yet, at last, this place is most amusing. They have
been eating me for days, and as they eat they carry away
the fear. I am becoming part of a vast empire of leaves
and minerals. It is a kind of opulent dozing, and I find
to my surprise that I am irreducible. Occasionally I hear
the sound of people above me, mourning, and one day
an old gaffer fell into a marsh, crying out my name. Most
amusing. I'll try to reach him.

5

Basho is dead and his ideas.
What can a woman make of that?
Burn his clothes, cover his ears.
Carve on his tomb of modest slate
He was my husband. Fifty years.

AN INTERVIEW WITH BASHO

Basho: 'The eye by way of the field mouse to the comma; the tooth by way of the hiccup to the dream.'

Interviewer: *What was that?*

B: Nothing. Let's move under the damson tree. It catches the light beautifully about this time. Look at the way the fishboat pushes its arrowhead slowly across the lake. And if you listen carefully you can hear the creak of its rowlocks.

Int: *When did you first start writing?*

B: It's like the pain in your back. It's hard to tell when it got there.

Int: *Can you remember what prompted you to begin?*

B: Pigeons.

Int: *Pigeons?*

B: And cormorants. I've always envied cormorants. Though eating raw fish is hardly my idea of a decent meal. Imagine that frantic wriggling in your throat. Ugh!

Int: *What was it about the pigeons?*

B: The way they flap round like old rags. The angles they make in the wind. There's nothing very beautiful about them. Piglets of the air I call them. But I like the way they launch themselves like a suicide from a ledge then, just when you think they're going to fall to pieces, they suddenly fly.

Int: *What does all that have to do with poetry though?*

B: One line for an image, one image to the line.

Int: *What does that mean?*

B: I'm not sure. I'm working at it.

Int: *Let's go back to the pigeons.*

B: Very well. I'm back.

Int: *I still don't understand.*

B: What don't you understand?

Int: *How they got you started. Pigeons and poetry. I don't get it.*

B: In one language I can think of there are over fifty words for the notion of 'to tremble'— all of them carrying a slight but distinct nuance. Our language is lazy; we have only three or four. Which means that when we come to the flight of the pigeon we are almost completely inarticulate. Yet you can count at least 81 characteristic movements—counter-turn, bank, the wing-tip stand and the side-slip—all kinds of movements. The thing is to find a verb for them and the emotions they awaken. The whole language a kind of verb.

Int: *Have you been exclusively concerned with pigeons all your life?*

B: Heavens, no! That was only a start. Lately I have been studying the rhythm of sea-weed, the texture of black bulls. Lots of things.

Int: *Does the study of linguistics help a writer?*

B: Linguistics talks of phonemes. My basic unit is the croneme.

Int: *The croneme? What kind of a thing is that?*

B: A croneme is the unit of concentration, resonance, opulence and nonsense.

Int: *Can you give an example?*

B: Any word in a good poem is a croneme. One of our modern masters has a narrative which at one point contains the amazing sentence: *So.* In that word he captures very accurately one moment of the pigeon's flight—a tragic moment as it happens: a young boy has just lost his hand and the poet writes, *So.* Very curious. A damned cheek, really.

Int: *But* So *is a phoneme, isn't it?*

B: Maybe. But it's a croneme as well.

Int: *I'm afraid you've lost me.*

B: Don't worry, this is difficult stuff. Break yourself off a plum. They're quite delicious.

Int: *No thanks. Bad digestion. I have to live exclusively off bean curds.*

B: Bean curds! Poor man—even the look of bean curds . . Well, never mind, let's get on . . .

Int: *Do you think that this is a bad century for a writer to live in?*

B: It certainly is. All centuries are bad. A few years ago
in the South someone unearthed a tablet about three
thousand years old. On it was an inscription from a father
to a son which read, 'Take care son, things are going to
hell. The end of civilization is near.' There have always
been gloomy people. We need them for comic relief.

Trouble is that gloominess is nowadays a social obligat-
ation. Ask a teacher how his students are doing. 'Idiots,'
he replies. 'I work myself sick trying to get the simplest
things into them . . the young are falling apart.' And
everybody says, *Yes, yes, it's awful isn't it?* Or you go
down to the fish market and ask about the catch and the
fishmonger says, 'Almost nothing, the lake's fished out.
We're going to starve . . .' And he nods his head and his fat
cheeks wobble. It's a kind of convention.

Int: *Do you think the schools are to blame?*

B: Perhaps. But schools have always been bad as well.
It's unrealistic to expect them to be otherwise. Mediocre
and safe views are the staple of schools. There's been no
essential change in that for thousands of years. But there is
a difference nowadays. Stupidity used to be accepted as one
of the hazards. Now we celebrate it— enthrone it, even.
There's such an accumulation of printed rubbish and such
an efficient bureaucracy that we can't get out from under
it. It's become *de rigueur* to be gloomy and stupid.

Int: *What about the teaching of poetry?*

B: Universal literacy has bred a generation of deaf-mutes.
They can *see* all right. But the other senses are asleep. So
the whole question of the meaning of a poem has been
reduced to one dimension:

Along the rough rock,
  an ant staggers under his load:
He's brought the beetle low, but the
  huge wing pins him down.

To read that correctly you have to get the accents right.
Otherwise you make nonsense of it.

Int: *But you yourself spoke of nonsense as the fourth charact-
eristic of your croneme—now it seems you're reviling it .*

B: Ho, you've pinned me! But watch out, I shall shake
you off! The croneme itself is nonsense. I just made it up
while we were talking.

Int: You *mean I shouldn't believe in it?*

B: Oh no, you *should* believe in it —it's very serious.
There are two kinds of nonsense—the nonsense of poetry
and the nonsense of nonsense. 'The lamplight falls on all
fours on the grass .' is probably the first kind—though
that's a problematical example, I admit. And if I gave you
the 81 poems on the flight of the pigeon you'd have
a hell of a time deciding which is which. I did, I can
assure you.

Int: You *mean you've written them? I've never seen a copy.
Where are they?*

B: I burned them. And the pigeons go on flying.

Int: *How does one tell nonsense from nonsense?*

B: A marvelous question to end with — and look, my
wife is bringing us tea. Lacking a harlot there's nothing

like jasmine tea, don't you think? And by the way, I should have added a fifth notion to the croneme.

Int: *What's that?*

B: Luck. But there's nowhere to put it. Croneme-*l*. What kind of a word would that make? Let's move out into the sun. Ah, look at that — the steam from our teacups is dissolving the mountain!

Postlude: A Sentimental Elegy

I wish at least that I could die tonight:
Nothing goes right,
All goes right.

I know the central trope reads 'born to die.'
Pains in my chest
And the crib
Rocking.

Flies bang their
Silly heads.

Who will conciliate?
And what to reconcile?

Sad, yet tipped with humor,
   the moments edge over
   the moments edge
   the moments
   the
   the

from

BASHO'S 81 POEMS
ON THE MOODS AND MODES
OF THE PIGEON

Bugged by the landlords,
the hard-beaked sparrows,
we take our stand
behind the shit-banks
on the Bank of England.

g

y

i

n

f

l

n

o   s

i   e

g

p

t^o

in

up

breaks

barn window

through the empty

smoke pours
a stream of whirring

Dog yaps

These days of wind

I am no better

than a snapped umbrella

stay low, fatty,
you're coming unglued.

roucou-ler

a thousand times

the sound goes round

the barn

rou-cou

rou-ou

rou-cou rou-ler

soon our language will be found

meanwhile

these idiot syllables

will have to do

will do   will do

They're packing horse-dung in a pile.
The horses cannot understand it.

Your tires
Kick out pebbles,
My bomb-body
Waddles across your
Raked gravel.
You say I'm common
As burdock, crabweed—

But when this barn's
Burned and eaten
Around your absence
Our wings will make
Rough music.

We bubble like pools of porridge.
Hyde Park Corner.
We've heard it all:

Politics. The art of the
Crunchable.

Ice in our wings:

our metal bodies

utterly still

the moon

wheeling slowly

around the empty farm

A white cat crunching wing-bones
Eyes me from the granary floor.
Look to your onions, arrogant bum:
Lost in your greedy delirium
With pigeon-lice pricking your skin
You're only a bundle of burning fur —
A complex meal that eats itself,
An ecological sewer.

Dear Cat: I'm heading South.
I've my own lice to lead.

P.S. Die. Immediately.

All the ladies are fat again,
some so pleased with themselves
they bounce their eggs down

thirty feet.

A startled pigeon
Jumped into my eye, and snapped

The lid.

(sings)

IF I HAD THE WINGS

OF A SWALLOW

That way, madness.

They've blocked us out of the barn
With chicken wire and chunks of wood.

Above us the vast October sky.

O the beasts of the earth have their lairs
And the Son of Man has overstuffed chairs
And a wide sweet-smelling bed—
But this night
Under the horrible, thin starlight
The Son of Pigeon
Has nowhere to lay his head.

A sound as real
And round as a pebble,
A big song bouncing off the moon
The rise, the roll, the carol, the creation:
That kind of thing.

Nothing except this dry click in my throat.

Comes a moment in the affairs of Pigeon
When almost everything seems dung.
The reason for the vision's plain:
Almost everything here *is* dung.

I have been thinking about dogs.
No dog thinks of me.
In this respect I am wasting my life.

Saturday: a blue sound
full of pigeons

Here's Basho again.
Mooching about in his dirty robe.
What a bore . . .
Fancies he's inventing us
With all those words.
Hey Basho, take that!

It rhymes.

Hard to think
with this idiot moonlight
pouring down:
horses in the yard
can't shake their shadows,
warm engines running,
engines and insects
throbbing under the moon.

Each thing fastened to its shadow.

Most of the statements
my feathers make
stop short.

Like that.

Notes on The Basho Poems

Not only the plan but a good deal of the original imagery was suggested by a student whose haiku lacked a syllable. This book is the missing syllable.

★

The Penguin edition of Basho's diaries, which I have not read, has a number of pages missing.

★

There has been some speculation about the identity of Basho. Some have claimed that he is the re-incarnation of the ancient Japanese poet who is at present living near Dreck, Missouri—which, of course, is nonsense.

★

Basho is a fictional character but his wife is real.

Hackberry Hollow
Northfield, Minnesota
1972 & 1981

WHEN THE IRISH BULLS ROLLED OVER

or

Basho's Brief but Penetrating Study
of
You Know,
the
Whole Schmoo

(1988)

for

Seamus Deane

*in honor
of his escape
to and from Northfield
in the Fall
of 1988*

Stuck.
Black block. Until.
Stuck. Word-rock.
World-rock. Stuck
Smack-center, white page.
Until.
Slow days.
Snow haze.
Outside, metal leaves
On dead wood.
Enamel sky.
No green blood in
Hacked stumps bogged in muck,
Nor red, in veins
Pulsing. Head, heart.
Stuck. Until

Seamus rolls in with his broguish grin
And roguish roiling eye.

Can you play petanques, Seamus ?

Petanques ? Don't know, never tried.

Plays it all the same, a doozer
First time up and me the loser
All along the gravel track,
He with a street-wise
Gleam in his eyes,
And ram-rod back,
Kissing the piglet on the nose each time and me
As happy as a beetle in a rooster's beak,
Coming unstuck as Irish luck
Leaks out of him, like steam.
Steam us, Seamus, beam on us, and cream us.

Can you play the cello, Seamus, Seamus ?

Click, and the big ball sits on the little pig's head.

Cello ? Don't know, never tried.

Unstuck. Go home, Seamus, sent to shame us.

(And me with my Celtic ancestors, and all.)

★

Wine, as I remember.

Wine: September and November.
(All October quasi-sober)
Hammered at the word-bench
While the grackles gargled and then
Carked off to the South—
And there was Seamus doubled over
(Gloucester at Dover)
With words, troubled chap, herds
Of headlong clobber-footed
Cattle clabbering in his brain
Mooing for attention and the screen too packed
For any one mind to ride their backs.

Seamus, alone,
Staring at
Green snow clanking down.
Stuck.
White rock.

Blank horizon rubbing blanker sky.

★

O Seamus, you will never frame us,
Said the Irish bull.
We've watched you growing famous, Seamus,
Seamus, you're a fool;

Fool for leaving Dublin, Seamus,
More fool to end up here
Where everyone's an ignoramus
And ice grows in your ear.

We fart on exiles when they blame us
For holding to our ground—
Ones like you that drift off, Seamus:
You, and Ezra Pound.

At this distance you won't tame us,
Not from Gitchee Gumee
Pack your bags for Dublin, Seamus—
Or we'll quatch your quoomie. ★

★

He thought it was Mnemosyne at first because the edges of the black pool suddenly took form and the still, unthinkable center, and all the time peculiar light from a woman's body, light fuming from the page, and there they were again, the pool, and her flesh blazing from the library book, yes, it must have been because his hand was racing now trying to catch the flicker and the stillness, because a dangerous energy simmered in his fingers, the pages laughing as they grew and rhythms he had carried all his life and never known before, gathering, and the bulls all sleeping now, every single one of them.

It must have been.

Because the clock said midnight in the depth of noon.

The small boy and the serious man together, doubled over, wondering at it all.

★

Brown voice
Warm as tweed.
Word-wise:
Green surprise
Of adjective
That kicks its noun
Upside-down:
The long light
Over stones
Over sour bones
Of history
For a moment clear.

This also work
Dignified
As a dug ditch,
And difficult:
Keyboard tuned
To a pitch
Where it almost cracks.

No poetry
That cannot risk
Blackness
Terminal cell-block:
Novalis, Mandelstam.

Invisible work,
That the rock
In our minds
Might fly.

Northfield, Minnesota
November, 1988

* Note for Linguists

Quatch and *quoomie* are Australian words of Gaelic origin but unknown meaning.

BASHO PLAYS GOLF
(1997)

His brother
Calls him. *All right, son,*
You wanna

Play ?
                    Play what ?
(It's early, even
The blue jays

Are snoring.)
Don't give me that, his
Brother snaps.

You left-wing
Intellectuals
Make me sick.

There's ONE game.
Besides, you're too old
For the others.

Myrtle Beach.
Six o'clock. It's three
Hundred bucks.

Be ready.

For nine, or eighteen?
He asks but

The phone's gone
Dead. He turns over,
Tries to sleep,

But his mind
Flares with fantasies:
Tom Lehman

Steering a
Slice around trees, and
Between geese;

Controlled fades;
A long draw that skims
The bunker.

He's flying.
That evening cleans his
Dusty clubs

Practices
In the kitchen — long
Floating drives.

★

Up at four,
Waiting. They set off
In darkness.

Like fishing
He says.
             What ?
                      Even
The ravens

Are rubbing
The sleep from their eyes.
Metaphors.

His brother's
Sour this morning.
                    Look

This is real

A real ball
A real club. And you.
No room for

Metaphors.
Right, he says, thinking:
The bastard,

I'll show him:
I'll be literal
As all get

-out. And mean.

First hole: he tees up
And squints hard.

He can't make
Out the fairway but
Swings, creams it.

Yeah — it's long
And high! His brother
Shakes his head.

Your ball is
Behind you. His tone's
Real neutral.

What ?
Behind
The clubhouse.
They find
It, swimming

In the pool
Surrounding the bronze
Statue of

Jack Nicklaus,
Officials swarming
Everywhere

Looking grave,
Snickering. *Two strokes for*
The fountain.

Sir, you must
Tee off again.
Thanks.
Myrtle Beach.

Hell with it!
First hole in thirteen.
His brother

Birdies it.
Stay calm, remember
The Buddha.

Next hole. Score:
Sixteen. Course record.
His grandson

Age four, could
Throw the thing up here
In five. Just

Concentrate.
Relax. Swing easy.
Stop thinking.

Concentrate !
By now he's hating
Everyone.

At the ninth
His brother's lead is
Forty-three.

He conducts
A long Socratic
Dialogue

With himself;
Exquisite, balanced.
He recalls

The complete
Metaphysical
Tradition,

East and West:
Madame Blavatsky,
Lotus and

Rose; recalls
The Thousand Things,
Then blurts out

Screw all this!
He kisses all the
Officials

And stalks off.
Even the squirrels
Stop to watch.

I love you.
He waves grandly. *IT'S*
A GREAT GAME!

In the car
His brother's face is
Grooved granite.

Three hundred
Bucks, and you make a
Fool of me.

Three hundred
Bucks, and you wanna
Quit early

Like a sick
Dog.
          Careful with your
Similes.

Aw, shut up.
You think too much — or
Not enough.
                    (pause)

In Japan
It's three thousand bucks.
What ?
                    Nothing.

He feels good
Now. He's decided:
Poetry

Not golf. He
Swells with resolve, and
Quietly,

Hums himself
Home with a pleasing
Little rune:

Golf's a dream
Will make a sane man
Very sick;

Metaphors
Might be lethal but
The poison's

Not so quick.

Index of Titles

Index of First Lines

For almost three decades Australian-born writer Keith Harrison taught English, Creative Writing and Environmental Studies at Carleton College, Northfield, Minnesota, where he was Professor of English and Writer-in-residence. Now in retirement, he divides his time between Australia and America, seeking, when possible, the steepest meridian of the sun. He has published many books of poetry and translation, the latest being a verse translation of *Sir Gawain and the Green Knight* (Oxford World's Classics). He is represented in more than a dozen national anthologies in Australia, England and America, and his work has been printed, broadcast and performed widely throughout the English-speaking world, **CHANGES: *New & Collected Poems, 1962-2002,*** is scheduled for publication in 2002.

Printed in the United States
68662LVS00002B/19